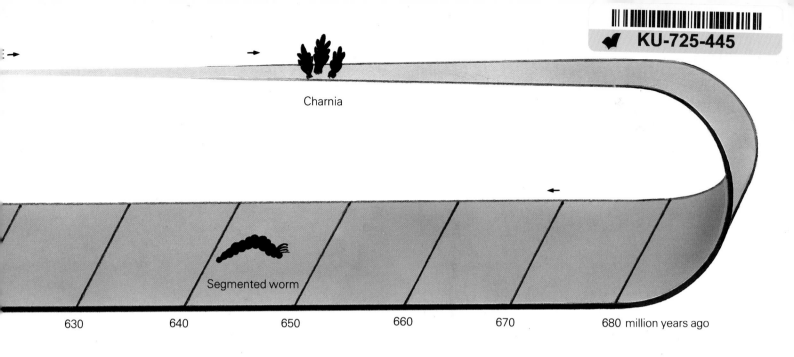

Charnia

Segmented worm

630 640 650 660 670 680 million years ago

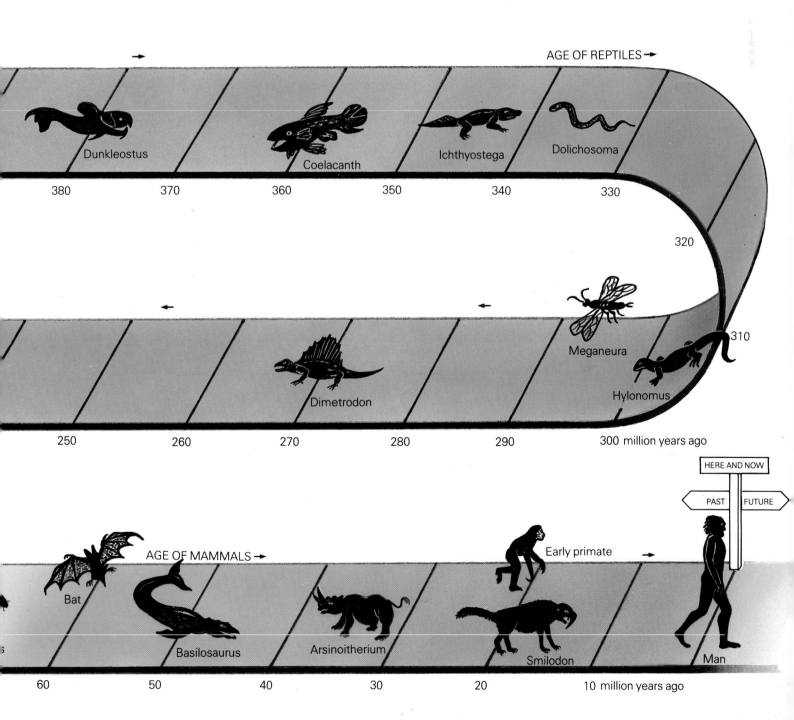

AGE OF REPTILES →

Dunkleostus

Coelacanth

Ichthyostega

Dolichosoma

380 370 360 350 340 330

320

Meganeura

310

Dimetrodon

Hylonomus

250 260 270 280 290 300 million years ago

HERE AND NOW

PAST FUTURE

Bat

AGE OF MAMMALS →

Early primate

Basilosaurus

Arsinoitherium

Smilodon

Man

60 50 40 30 20 10 million years ago

ISBN 0 86112 665 3
© Brimax Books Ltd 1990, All rights reserved.
Published by Brimax Books Ltd, Newmarket, England 1990.
Reprinted 1993.
This edition previously appeared as two separate volumes,
Dinosaurs and *Animals from the Dawn of Time*.
Produced by Mandarin Offset.
Printed in China.

THE
BIG BOOK
OF DINOSAURS

Written by Stephen Attmore
Illustrated by David A. Hardy

Diagrams by David A. Hardy and Brian Rhoden

Brimax Books · Newmarket · England

Contents

When was the Dawn of Time?

The story of life on Earth goes back to the very dawn of time – over 3,500 million years ago.

It began with the microscopic life-forms that came into being in the orange-coloured 'soup' that made up the seas that covered the planet.

From that starting point many different forms of life developed. Some, like the dinosaurs have disappeared along the way. A few have survived and exist today much as they were thousands or even millions of years ago; others have undergone changes as part of the process of evolution. Together they form the wide range of animal species alive today.

This book traces the development of animal life from the very beginning, showing which forms of life dominated the world at different stages. Within the book, those animals featured in boxes are surviving examples or possible descendants of prehistoric species. Those animals featured in **bold** type are illustrated.

How to say the names of the prehistoric creatures

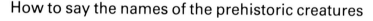

algae	al-gee	hyracotherium	hi-rak-oh-therr-ee-um
archaeopteryx	ark-ee-op-ter-iks	icarosaurus	ik-arrow-sor-us
australopithecus	ostra-loh-pith-eek-us	ichthyornis	ik-thi-ornis
brachiosaurus	brak-ee-oh-sor-us	ichthyostega	ik-thi-oh-steeg-ah
charnia	char-nee-ah	mastodonsaurus	mass-toe-don-sor-us
cladoselache	clad-oh-se-lak-ee	meganeura	meg-ah-nure-ah
coelacanth	see-la-kanth	megatherium	meg-a-therr-ee-um
coelophysis	see-lo-fy-sis	megazostrodon	meg-ah-zos-troh-don
coelurus	see-loor-us	megistotherium	meg-isto-therr-ee-um
compsognathus	komp-so-na-thus	paramys	pah-rah-mis
cynognathus	sino-na-thus	podopteryx	pod-op-ter-iks
deinonychus	die-non-ike-us	proganochelys	pro-gan-oh-kel-iss
deinosuchus	die-no-sook-us	pteranodon	ter-a-no-don
diadectes	die-ah-dek-tees	pteraspis	ter-asp-iss
diatryma	die-ah-try-ma	quetzalcoatlus	kwet-zal-kote-lus
dinichthys	din-ik-thees	ramapithecus	ram-ah-pith-eek-us
diplocaulus	dip-loh-cor-lus	rhamphorhynchus	ram-for-in-kus
dolichosoma	dol-ik-oh-som-ah	saltoposuchus	salt-oh-poss-ook-us
dunkleostus	dunk-lee-oss-tis	scutosaurus	skew-toe-sor-us
dryopithecus	dry-oh-pith-eek-us	stegoceras	steg-oss-er-as
echidna	e-kid-na	synthetoceras	sin-thet-oss-er-as
ellopos	ee-lop-oss	tanystropheus	tan-ee-strofe-ee-us
eryops	erri-ops	triceratops	try-ser-a-tops
eusthenopteron	yous-the-nop-terr-on	tuatara	twa-tar-a
hesperornis	hess-per-or-niss	tyrannosaurus	tie-ran-oh-sor-us
hylonomus	hi-lon-o-mus	uintatherium	win-tah-therr-ee-um

When did prehistoric animals first appear?

Tiny living things appeared on Earth 3500 million years ago. Remains of the earliest known creatures are found in rocks dating back nearly 600 million years. The first animals, which were simple fish, evolved about 530 million years ago.

About 200 million years later came the invasion of the land by the sea creatures that developed into amphibians. The age of the reptiles followed with the mighty dinosaurs pre-eminent for 160 million years. When they died out they gave way to birds and mammals. From among the mammals about 10 million years ago a small ape began to walk upright evolving eventually into the species homo sapiens – the human beings of today.

The Earth 600 million years ago

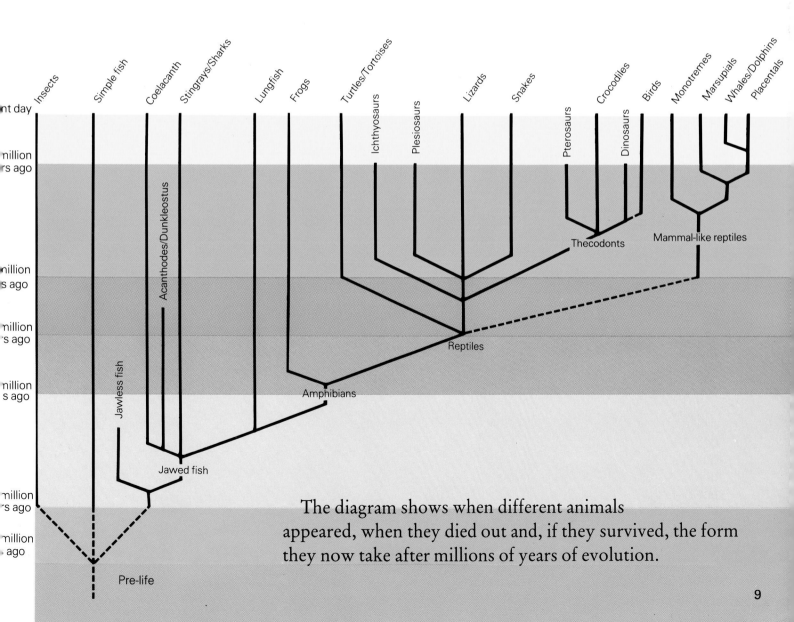

The diagram shows when different animals appeared, when they died out and, if they survived, the form they now take after millions of years of evolution.

The first forms of life

3,500–550 million years ago

4,500 million years ago, Earth was a very different planet to the one we live on today. The outer surface of the planet was gradually cooling as the crust slowly hardened. Thunderstorms shook the air and many volcanoes erupted. Thousands of years of rain created warm shallow oceans. The sun poured lethal radiation over the planet. There was no oxygen in the air.

Over millions of years the seas became an orange-coloured 'soup', full of chemicals that had been washed off the land. In this soup, small living things began to develop. These were single cells, called **bacteria** – the smallest and simplest forms of life. Some of these developed a green chemical, chlorophyll, to make their food. They used this and sunlight to convert carbon dioxide in the air into food. They also released oxygen into the air which is vital for all living things.

Over many millions of years the amount of oxygen increased, eventually forming a screen against the sun's rays. This is called ozone and it is what makes the sky look blue. Conditions were now right for more advanced life to begin.

Simple plants such as **blue-green algae** (1) were among the first forms to appear. The oldest known fossil is of algae, 3,400 million years old. Algae like this still survives today. You can see it on the top of ponds, making the surface look green. After about 2,500 million years, cells began to group themselves together to make very simple plants and animals. Here the cells eventually became heart, brain and muscles. **Jellyfish** (2) was an early animal. Fossilised remains in rocks have been dated as 600 million years old.

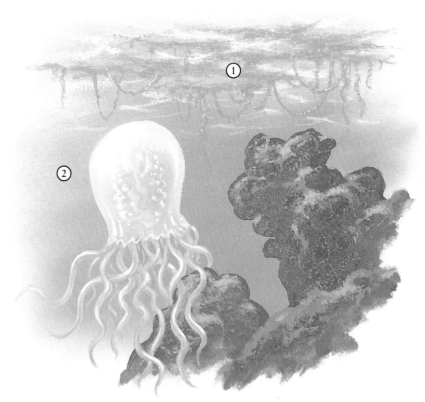

By about 570 million years ago many invertebrates (animals without backbones) were active on the sea-bed. There were worms, molluscs, sea-snails and arthropods. We know about these creatures from tracks, tunnels and prints of their bodies left in some rocks.

Spriggina (1) was a segmented worm. Its body was 5 cm (2 inches) long. The **trilobite** (2) was a large arthropod. Each segment on a trilobite's body had a pair of limbs which it used for walking, swimming, breathing and handling food. Trilobites died out about 250 million years ago. **Dentalium** (3) was a mollusc with a fleshy 'coat' and a hard shell. **Charnia** (4) was a soft coral fixed to the sea-bed, 40 cm (1⅓ ft) tall. **Sponges** (5) fixed themselves to a rock and filtered water for food.

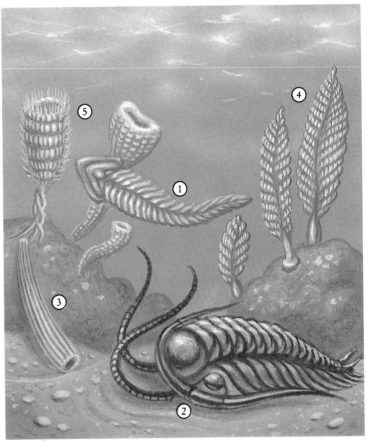

The fossilised remains of **sponges** have been found in rocks as much as 395 million years old. They have hardly changed since then. A living sponge is a sort of fleshy bag held up by a skeleton. For many years scientists thought sponges were plants. Then they realised that a sponge breathes and feeds. It draws in water through lots of little holes before removing tiny particles of food.

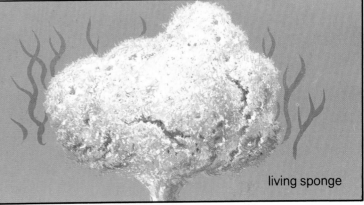

living sponge

11

From the sea to the land

550–345 million years ago

Let us go back to about 550 million years ago. From fossils found in a mudstone cliff in the Rocky Mountains in Canada it is possible to picture a scene under water. Here were some of the first animals which swam in the seas. All of the creatures were small with soft, jelly-like bodies. Some moved slowly, others were fixed to the sea-bed.

Sea-lilies (1) looked like strange plants. About 15 cm (6 inches) high, these animals swayed gently in the water. **Charnia** (2) looked like a bunch of feathers. **Sponges** (3) had simple bodies, open at the top. Drifting through the water were **flatworms** (4) and **jellyfish** (5). Crawling over the rocks, a **trilobite** (6) felt its way using a pair of long feelers. There were also **starfishes** (7), **worms** (8) and **lancelets** (9). Some of these creatures are unlike anything alive today.

About 400 million years ago the first plants appeared on land. Creatures such as spiders and millipedes began to live on land once the vegetation provided shelter and food.

The scene under water was very different. Some of the first sea creatures had died out, but others had developed and adapted to the changing conditions. The sea water was saltier. **Trilobites** (1) and **worms** (2) were everywhere. **Corals** (3) built great reefs. **Molluscs** (4) grazed on **algae** (5).

The major development during this period was the first appearance of a fish.

From the lancelet evolved the **jawless fish** (6). Its body armour saved this creature from being eaten by the '**sea scorpion**' (7). Jawed fish appeared several million years later. **Acanthodes** (8) was an eel-like 'spiny fish'. The giant **dunkleostus** (9) lurked on or near the sea-bed, seeking prey. None of these early forms of fish were very good at swimming.

The first fish

The **lancelet** is an odd creature that lives today in shallow seas. It is the direct descendant of the early invertebrate that evolved into fish. It moves by wriggling its very simple body. It has no head, no heart and no fins or limbs. The opening at the front end is ringed with feelers. Fossil remains of a lancelet were dated as 550 million years old.

True fish are vertebrates (animals with a backbone) that live in water. They breathe through gills. The oldest known vertebrate was **arandaspis** which lived about 500 million years ago. This fish was about 12 cm (4½ inches) long. It had no jaws or fins. The front half of its body was covered in scales.

The development of the first jawed fish was a dramatic event in animal evolution. Jaws enabled these creatures to eat larger items of food, especially other fish. **Acanthodes** swam in fresh-water rivers and lakes about 280 million years ago. It was about 30 cm (1 ft) long. Its big eyes were useful when hunting prey.

Dunkleostus, or dinichthys, was a large, fish-eating predator. There is no living creature like it. In its mouth, it had rows of bony picks and two pairs of fangs. The first of these creatures to evolve was probably only 50 cm (1⅔ ft) long. Over a period of 50 million years they developed into 9 m (30 ft) monsters.

lancelet

arandaspis

acanthodes

dunkleostus

Sharks and bony fish

About 350 million years ago, two different types of fish began to evolve. One group developed a skeleton of cartilage, instead of bone, which is lighter and softer. These creatures were the ancestors of sharks and rays. They could swim faster than other fish. In order to stay above the sea-bed they had to keep swimming, just like today's sharks. Sharks probably evolved from creatures like dunkleostus. **Cladoselache** was a prehistoric shark. This fierce killer had sharp teeth and was up to 2 m (6½ ft) in length.

The second group of fish kept their bony skeleton. They evolved a new way of breathing. Part of the stomach was separated off to form a lung or swim-bladder (air pouch). Lungfish like the **dipterus** had both gills and a lung. If the rivers dried up, they could breathe in air. Some prehistoric bony fish could fill their air pouches with gas produced from their blood. By controlling the amount of gas in the pouch, the fish held its position or moved up or down. It did not have to keep moving its tail.

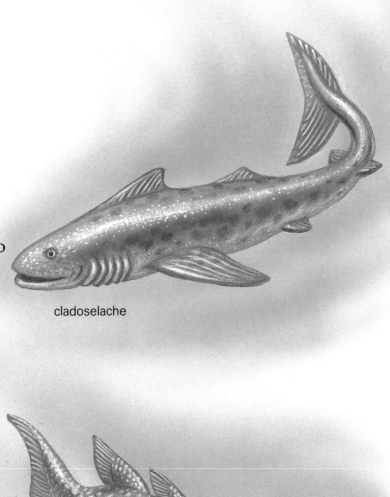

cladoselache

dipterus

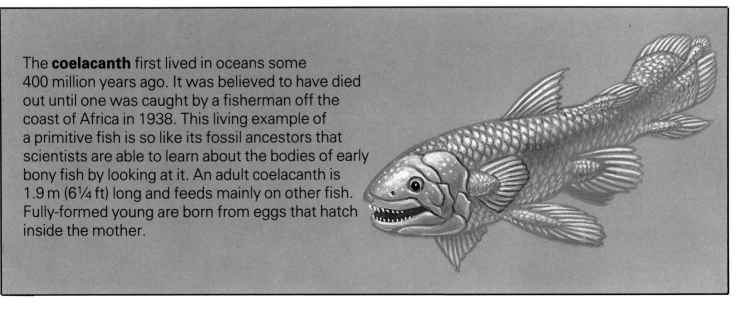

The **coelacanth** first lived in oceans some 400 million years ago. It was believed to have died out until one was caught by a fisherman off the coast of Africa in 1938. This living example of a primitive fish is so like its fossil ancestors that scientists are able to learn about the bodies of early bony fish by looking at it. An adult coelacanth is 1.9 m (6¼ ft) long and feeds mainly on other fish. Fully-formed young are born from eggs that hatch inside the mother.

The invasion of the land

An important stage in the history of life took place some 350 million years ago. In a fresh-water swamp some fish began to haul themselves out of the water and on to land. The **eusthenopteron** used its front pair of fins to pull itself through the mud. Its fins had a bony skeleton (a) that did not have to undergo much change to become the limb of an amphibian. Breathing was no problem for it had air pouches like lungs. A passage linked the nostrils with the roof of the mouth. This is a feature common to all land vertebrates. The eusthenopteron was less than 60 cm (2 ft) long.

There are several reasons why lungfish might have left the water. Perhaps there was not enough oxygen in the muddy water. Perhaps they were looking for food. Perhaps their pools dried up. Whatever the reason, these creatures became more and more skilful at moving and breathing out of water. They slowly evolved into amphibians, spending part of the time in water, part of the time on land. They became the first vertebrates with legs.

An early amphibian, **ichthyostega**, was about 1 m (3 ft) long and had a tail like a fish. The fin skeleton had lost some of the bones to become more like a hand (b). It had also formed an elbow. This amphibian probably spent most of the time in water.

a

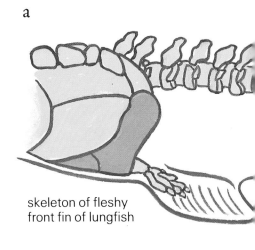

skeleton of fleshy
front fin of lungfish

b

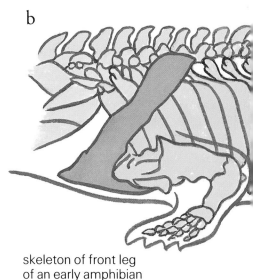

skeleton of front leg
of an early amphibian

eusthenopteron

ichthyostega

For the next 100 million years, the amphibians ruled the land. They adapted to the hot, dry conditions. Eyelids and tear glands developed to keep their eyes moist. Eventually amphibians began to produce a moisture which protected their skin and allowed them to stay out of water for longer. Some were large, like the **eryops** – 1.5 m (5 ft) in length. Its skeleton was stronger for life on land. This heavy amphibian fed on fish.

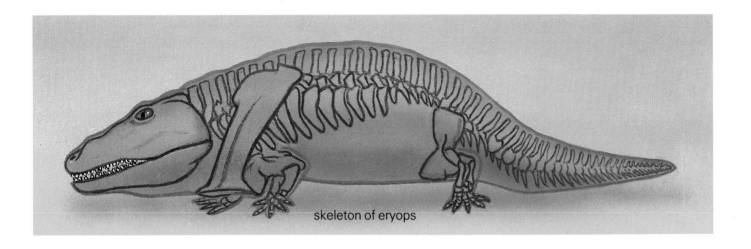

skeleton of eryops

Diplocaulus was the same size as ichthyostega. It lived in Texas, USA, and had strange 'horns' on the sides of its head. These may have helped the amphibian when swimming. They would also have made it difficult for predators to swallow it.

Mastodonsaurus was an amphibian that looked like a giant frog. It was over 3 m (10 ft) long. Its jaws were armed with sharp teeth.

Early reptiles

345–225 million years ago

The hot, wet climate resulted in the development of many plants on low-lying land. Swampy forests attracted all sorts of prehistoric animals. Amphibians evolved rapidly. Some were large, such as **eryops** (1). Others looked like newts or salamanders. Crawling in the rotting debris on the forest floor was **dolichosoma** (2). **Pantylus** (3) was an insect-eater. **Ichthyostega** (4) spent most of its time in water as did **diplocaulus** (5).

Arthropods like the **scorpion** (6) became more common. The largest ever land arthropod was a flat **millipede** (7) at 1.8 m (6 ft) long. It was during this period that the first true insects appeared. A **springtail** (8) was probably the first wingless insect. It lived in the soil and would flip into the air if scared. **Meganeura** (9) was the largest known winged insect. It had a wingspan of 70 cm (2¼ ft) and like today's dragonflies it was unable to fold its wings back. The first reptiles appeared at about 280 million years ago.

Key

1 eryops
2 dolichosoma
3 pantylus
4 ichthyostega
5 diplocaulus
6 scorpion
7 millipede
8 springtail
9 meganeura

For some 50 million years amphibians were the largest animals able to move on land. They adapted slowly to life on dry land and still had to return to water to breed. Reptiles were the first backboned animals to live entirely on land. From 280 to 225 million years ago, a number of reptiles evolved.

In the rocks of Texas, USA, there are fossils of several types of vertebrates. They are around 270 million years old. As you can see in the picture, wet-land amphibians looked like the dry-land reptiles. **Diadectes** (1) a wet-land amphibian, probably stayed close to water. It was the earliest known vertebrate to feed on plants. **Seymouria** (2) a dry-land reptile may have had a thick skin so that it could live in the desert. It only had to return to water to breed. The reptiles with huge 'sails' on their backs were **dimetrodons** (3).

Key

1 diadectes
2 seymouria
3 dimetrodon

The first reptiles

It is not clear which amphibians were the ancestors of reptiles. It is also not clear at which point in the history of life the developing amphibians became the first reptiles. What is known is that the most important change was the ability to lay a shelled egg. This stopped the eggs drying up after they were laid. Reptiles were now free to move away from the water. There were many more changes that helped these prehistoric animals to survive on land. Some of them are shown below.

Hylonomus was one of the first reptiles. It was 1 m (3¼ ft) long and lived in Canada. This insect-eater lived a life similar to modern lizards.

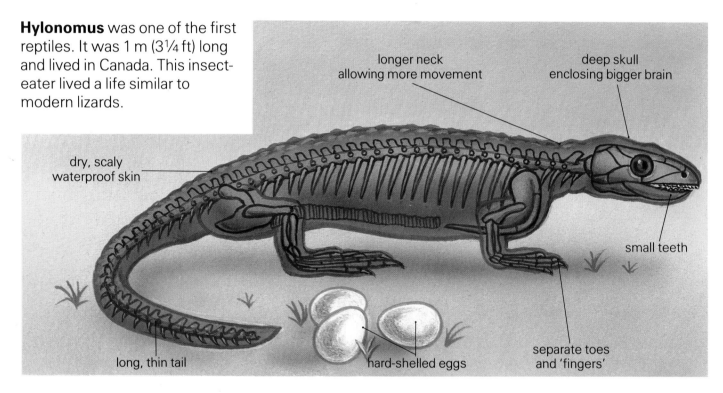

longer neck
allowing more movement

deep skull
enclosing bigger brain

dry, scaly
waterproof skin

small teeth

long, thin tail

hard-shelled eggs

separate toes
and 'fingers'

Another early reptile was **scutosaurus**. This big creature was a plant-eater. It was 2.4 m (8 ft) long and lived in Russia. Scutosaurus stood more upright than many reptiles.

A range of reptiles

Reptiles now began to invade new areas on land. In fact, they adapted to life in all parts of the world except the polar regions. Many different types developed. There were reptiles that walked, reptiles that swam, flying reptiles, running reptiles, giant reptiles and tiny reptiles, plant-eaters and meat-eaters.

Reptiles are cold-blooded animals that need heat from the sun to give them energy. **Dimetrodon** had long spines jutting from its backbone which supported a skin 'sail'. If it stood sideways to the early morning sun, many of the sun's rays hit the sail, warming the reptile's blood. This enabled it to attack prey that was still drowsy. To cool down, the dimetrodon stood with its back to the sun or in the shade, so that fewer rays hit the sail.

Proganochelys was the ancestor of the turtle. Like modern turtles, it had a heavy shell (a bony 'box' covered with horny plates). The shell was 60 cm (2 ft) long. Proganochelys was unable to pull its limbs, head or tail inside its shell. Instead these parts were protected by sharp spikes and bony knobs.

Icarosaurus was a 'flying' reptile that lived in North America. It did not really fly; it glided from tree to tree. Ribs extended from the body and were covered in skin, forming a pair of wings. The hind legs of icarosaurus were longer and stronger than its front legs. This suggests that this prehistoric lizard also ran on its two hind legs.

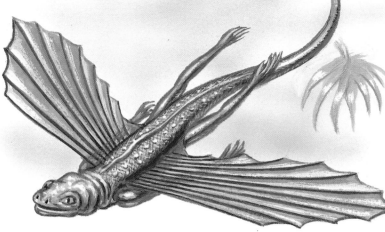

Tanystropheus was a very strange looking reptile indeed. It grew to 6 m (19½ ft) in length with a long but rather rigid neck. The young stayed on land but adults lived on the shore or in shallow waters. It probably used its long neck like a fishing rod to catch fish.

Sea reptiles

Many early reptiles adapted to a life in the open sea. The animals shown here did not actually live in the same seas or at the same time. **Ichthyosaurs** (1) were lizards that looked like modern dolphins. They had a body designed for swimming at fast speeds and they hunted in packs. Adult ichthyosaurs ate their young if there was no other food. Females gave birth to live young in the water. They could not crawl on land.

Mesosaurs (2) belonged to a family of sea lizards that seized food in sharp-toothed jaws. Fossil remains up to 8 m (26 ft) in length were uncovered in North America and New Zealand. Plesiosaurs (sea reptiles) developed into two main types. The short-necked **kronosaurus** (3) was 12 m (39 ft) long and lived near Australia. The 'snake-turtle' **elasmosaurus** (4) was up to 13 m (42½ feet) long and had over 70 neck bones. Its four flippers allowed it to make sharp turns and even swim backward but it could not dive. Elasmosaurus did not have to chase prey, it simply darted its head down into the water and grabbed passing fish. This North American reptile laid it eggs on the shore.

Reptiles rule

Lizards appeared some 230 million years ago. Apart from flying lizards and sea lizards, there were several prehistoric species living on land. Crocodiles and dinosaurs emerged from this group of large flesh-eaters. One of these, **desmatosuchus,** was 4 m (13 ft) long and had heavy skin armour. Its neck was also protected by horns.

Deinosuchus was the largest-ever crocodile at 16 m (52½ ft) long. It appeared some 140 million years ago. Fossils found in Texas show this reptile had huge jaws. It lurked in rivers and ambushed dinosaurs that came to drink. Nostrils on the top end of its snout enabled it to breathe while eating.

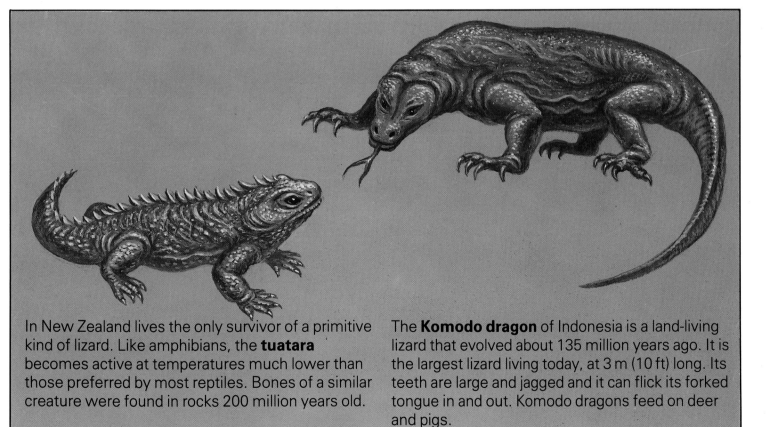

In New Zealand lives the only survivor of a primitive kind of lizard. Like amphibians, the **tuatara** becomes active at temperatures much lower than those preferred by most reptiles. Bones of a similar creature were found in rocks 200 million years old.

The **Komodo dragon** of Indonesia is a land-living lizard that evolved about 135 million years ago. It is the largest lizard living today, at 3 m (10 ft) long. Its teeth are large and jagged and it can flick its forked tongue in and out. Komodo dragons feed on deer and pigs.

What was a dinosaur?

For 160 million years dinosaurs were the largest and most frightening animals that ever lived on Earth. Some weighed almost as much as a blue whale, about 130 tonnes (127 tons) – yet others were no bigger than a chicken. However, dinosaurs died out 65 million years ago.

The term 'dinosaur' was first used in 1841. It is taken from the Greek word 'deinos' meaning 'terrible' and 'saur' meaning 'lizard'. The dinosaur's ancestors were reptiles that ran on their hind legs. Many of these reptiles looked like crocodiles with their legs held out sideways. Others had limbs that were underneath the body so that they could run faster. Some developed large hind legs and short front legs. They used their hind legs for running and their front legs for grasping food.

tyrannosaurus rex

How to say the names of the dinosaurs in this book:

allosaurus	al-lo-sor-us	mastodonsaurus	mass-toe-don-sor-us
anatosaurus	an-at-oh-sor-us	megalosaurus	meg-a-lo-sor-us
ankylosaurus	an-kil-oh-sor-us	micropachycephalosaurus	my-kroh-pak-ee-sef-alo-sor-us
apatosaurus	a-pat-oh-sor-us	ornithomimus	or-nith-oh-mime-us
archaeopteryx	ark-ee-op-ter-iks	ornithosuchus	or-nith-oh-sook-us
barosaurus	barrow-sor-us	oviraptor	oh-vee-rap-tor
betasuchus	bee-ta-sook-us	pachycephalosaurus	pak-ee-sef-alo-sor-us
brachiosaurus	brak-ee-oh-sor-us	parasaurolophus	pah-rah-sor-ol-oh-fus
camptosaurus	kamp-toe-sor-us	placodus	plak-oh-dus
cetiosaurus	ket-ee-oh-sor-us	plateosaurus	plat-ee-oh-sor-us
coelophysis	see-lo-fy-sis	plesiosaur	ple-see-oh-sor
coelurus	see-loor-us	podopteryx	pod-op-ter-iks
compsognathus	komp-so-na-thus	protoceratops	pro-toe-ser-ah-tops
corythosaurus	korr-ee-tho-sor-us	psittacosaurus	sit-a-ko-sor-us
cynognathus	sino-na-thus	pteranodon	ter-a-no-don
deinonychus	die-non-ike-us	pterosaur	ter-oh-sor
diplodocus	dip-loh-doe-kus	quetzalcoatlus	kwet-zal-kote-lus
dromiceiomimus	drom-ick-eye-oh-mime-us	rhamphorhynchus	ram-for-in-kus
dryosaurus	dri-oh-sor-us	saltoposuchus	salt-oh-poss-ook-us
elasmosaurus	ee-laz-mo-sor-us	saurolophus	sor-ol-oh-fus
euparkeria	you-park-er-ee-ah	saurornithoides	sor-or-nith-oy-dees
fabrosaurus	fab-ro-sor-us	sinosaurus	sy-no-sor-us
hypselosaurus	hip-sel-oh-sor-us	spinosaurus	spy-no-sor-us
hypsilophodon	hip-sil-off-od-on	staurikosaurus	stor-ik-oh-sor-us
iguanodon	ih-gwan-oh-don	stegoceras	steg-oss-er-as
kronosaurus	kro-no-sor-us	stegosaurus	steg-o-sor-us
lagosuchus	lag-oh-sook-us	styracosaurus	sty-rak-oh-sor-us
lesothosaurus	less-oh-toe-sor-us	teratosaurus	ter-a-toe-sor-us
lambeosaurus	lam-ee-oh-sor-us	triceratops	try-ser-a-tops
lystrosaurus	lie-stro-sor-us	tyrannosaurus	tie-ran-oh-sor-us
maiasaura	my-er-sor-ah		

When did dinosaurs roam the Earth?

The history of life on Earth is divided into three parts. It is the middle section that is known as the Age of Dinosaurs. Dinosaurs began to appear on Earth about 225 million years ago. They continued to breed and adapt to their environment over the next 160 million years.

If one year represents the time that there has been life on Earth, then the first dinosaurs did not appear until around December 8th and died out December 24th. The first human beings were born late in the evening of December 31st.

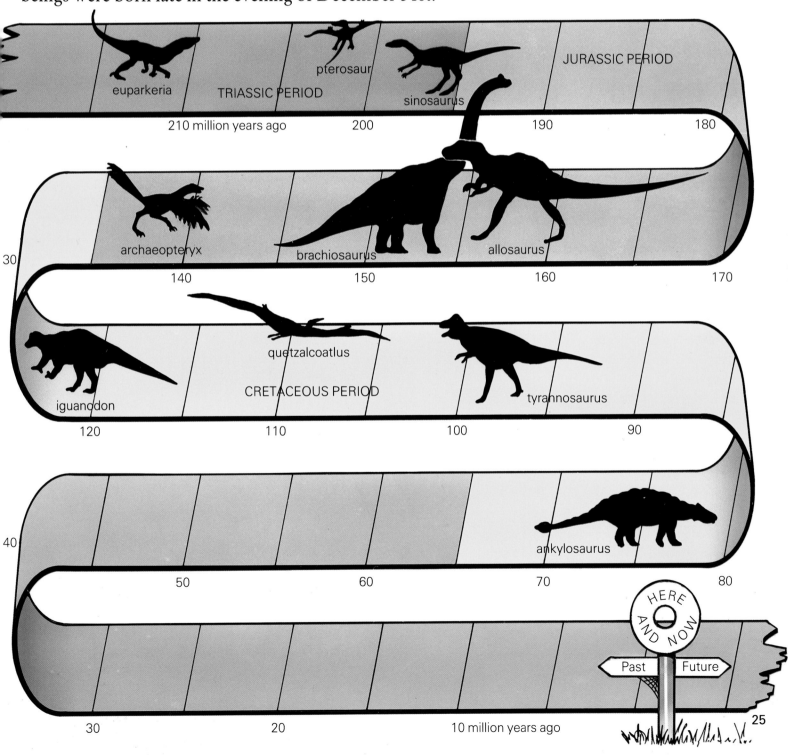

euparkeria

TRIASSIC PERIOD

pterosaur

sinosaurus

JURASSIC PERIOD

210 million years ago   200   190   180

archaeopteryx

brachiosaurus

allosaurus

30

140   150   160   170

iguanodon

quetzalcoatlus

CRETACEOUS PERIOD

tyrannosaurus

120   110   100   90

40

ankylosaurus

50   60   70   80

HERE AND NOW

Past   Future

30   20   10 million years ago

How dinosaurs evolved

Dinosaurs evolved from swimming reptiles (1) who hunted their prey in water. They swam by waggling their long, strong tails. To set off they pushed down and back with their hind legs which were longer and more powerful than their front limbs.

Over a long period of time – several million years – some of these reptiles took to living on the land mainly to find new sources of food and to avoid predatory fish. Most could not walk as upright as a dog, but used their limbs to lift their bodies off the ground (a). They probably looked like trotting crocodiles (2). At feeding and breeding times they returned to the water.

From such reptiles came creatures like the tiny **euparkeria** (3) which was only 1 m (3¼ ft) long. It walked on land on all fours lifting its body higher off the ground (b). As its short front legs made running difficult, the euparkeria sprinted by

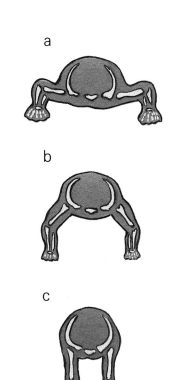

a

b

c

evolution of hip position

26

rearing up on its long hind legs. It used its very long tail to balance as it darted from place to place.

The **lagosuchus** (4) was given its name by scientists because of the speed at which it moved. Lagosuchus means 'hare crocodile'. This small creature also walked on all fours but ran on its hind legs only. Both the euparkeria and the lagosuchus were flesh-eating creatures, feeding on animals smaller than themselves. The **ornithosuchus** (5) was another flesh-eating hunter. It was about 3 m (9¾ ft) long.

True dinosaurs had a much improved stance with hind legs held straight down below the body (c). This helped dinosaurs like **staurikosaurus** (6) to outrun both prey and rivals. These dinosaurs were therefore more dangerous than their reptile ancestors. It is likely that the number of dinosaurs on Earth increased at a much quicker rate than other animals because they could run faster. The largest plant-eating dinosaurs could escape from predators and the meat-eating dinosaurs could catch and kill the slower moving animals.

key
1 lizard-like reptile
2 crocodile-like ancestor
   of the dinosaur
3 euparkeria
4 lagosuchus
5 ornithosuchus
6 staurikosaurus

Life in the Triassic Period

Earth – 225 million years ago, at the start of the Triassic Period.

As the picture shows, Earth was very different when the first dinosaurs lived on it. The land masses were joined together. Dinosaurs and other animals could roam for thousands of miles in search of food.

The first part of the Age of Dinosaurs is known as the Triassic Period. This lasted for about 35 million years and began about 225 million years ago.

Perhaps the most amazing thing about life on Earth in the Age of Dinosaurs was the climate. Everywhere was warm – all the time. Imagine summer lasting for millions of years. Although there were some mountains and volcanoes, most of the land was flat. There were many marshes and swamps, covered with a variety of trees and plants. One unusual tree called pleuromeia was 2 m (7 ft) high and had tufts of leaves near the top of its thick stalk.

It was during the Triassic Period that the first dinosaurs appeared. Reptiles began to adjust to a way of life on land. Along the shores waddled reptiles such as the **placodus**. This animal lived on land but returned to the sea in search of food. The **lystrosaurus** was a mammal-like reptile. It looked like a

baby hippo. The **cynognathus** was a hairy carnivore (meat-eater) about the size of a wolf.

The mammal-like reptiles were gradually replaced by early dinosaurs such as **euparkeria** and the **saltoposuchus** which was only 87 cm (2¾ ft) long. It ran on the toes of its hind legs, using its very long tail to help it balance. The **lagosuchus** was a small speedy, flesh-eating dinosaur.

Towards the end of the Triassic Period larger dinosaurs evolved. One of the biggest was a herbivore (plant-eater) called **plateosaurus**. The **ornithosuchus, staurikosaurus, teratosaurus** and **sinosaurus** were all carnivores. Above their heads gliding reptiles moved from tree to tree and the first **pterosaurs** flew by on skin wings.

key
1 placodus	6 lagosuchus	11 sinosaurus
2 lystrosaurus	7 plateosaurus	12 gliding lizard
3 cynognathus	8 ornithosuchus	13 pterosaur
4 euparkeria	9 staurikosaurus	
5 saltoposuchus	10 teratosaurus	

Life in the Jurassic Period

Earth – 165 million years ago, during the Jurassic Period.

The continents slowly drifted apart over millions of years. Fossil bones of the same type of dinosaur are now being uncovered in different continents around the world.

The Jurassic Period lasted for 50 million years. There was a great increase in the number of animals in the water, on land and in the air. By the end of the Period, dinosaurs were the rulers of the animal kingdom. Some had grown to enormous sizes and weights. The ground shook as they moved along.

The climate everywhere was warm and moist. There were coral reefs and lagoons along many coasts. Plants grew more thickly, including many cycads (palm-like plants with coloured fruits and cones).

A variety of dinosaurs evolved to feed on the many plants available. Small dinosaurs munched the fungi and ferns at ground level. Slim dinosaurs chewed the leaves a little higher up. The **dryosaurus** was one of the biggest of these. The **camptosaurus** and **stegosaurus** could rear up on their hind legs to strip leaves off the lower branches of the taller trees. Giant dinosaurs like **diplodocus, brachiosaurus** and **cetiosaurus** ate the leaves too high for the others to reach.

There were also many hunters on the prowl. **Coelurus** was about the length of an adult human. It used its long hind legs for speedy running. Perhaps this scavenger tore flesh off other dinosaurs and mammals killed by larger carnivores such as the **allosaurus**.

Above the heads of the ground-living creatures flapped 'winged dinosaurs'. They had fragile wings of skin and bone. When **archaeopteryx** and **rhamphorhynchus** took to the air, they probably flew slowly and clumsily. They were too big to fly far.

key
 1 dryosaurus
 2 camptosaurus
 3 stegosaurus
 4 diplodocus
 5 brachiosaurus
 6 cetiosaurus
 7 coelurus
 8 allosaurus
 9 archaeopteryx
10 rhamphorhynchus

Life in the Cretaceous Period

Earth – 100 million years ago, in the middle of the Cretaceous Period.

The continents are further apart. Seas separate the land masses and the climate is becoming more varied.

This was the last period in the Age of Dinosaurs. It lasted 70 million years, ending around 65 million years ago. During this time dinosaurs reached their peak and then mysteriously vanished from the face of the Earth.

In the Cretaceous Period many modern types of animal and plant appeared for the first time. There was a much greater variety of plants and trees. Flowering plants multiplied and spread. The climate was warm and wet ranging from very hot at the Equator to warm in the north.

There were many more plant-eating dinosaurs than meat-eaters. These evolved with teeth designed for chewing the new tough-leaved plants. They ranged in size from small two-footed dinosaurs to four-legged giants. The **micropachycephalosaurus** of China has one of the longest names but one of the shortest bodies of any dinosaur. Its

body was about 50 cm (20 ins) long. At the other end of the scale, the **apatosaurus** was still making the ground shake as it plodded across the plains of North America. This huge dinosaur was probably 21 m (70 ft) from nose to tip of tail.

Each creature had its own special feeding ground. The armour-plated **ankylosaurus** kept to higher, drier land. Duckbills such as the **corythosaurus** and **parasaurolophus** ate so much that they cleared areas completely. **Triceratops** roamed the plains in herds while **hypsilophodon** lived in forest glades. This left room for the ostrich dinosaurs like **betasuchus**. The massive **tyrannosaurus rex** fed on dead or injured dinosaurs.

Overhead flew the largest pterosaur, quetzalcoatlus at 12 m (39 ft) from wing tip to wing tip. The smaller **pteranodon** of North America had a wingspan of 8 m (26 ft). It spent most of its life in the air. There were also some species of true birds. **Gulls** and **wader birds** appeared for the first time during the Cretaceous Period.

key
1 micropachycephalosaurus
2 apatosaurus
3 ankylosaurus
4 corythosaurus
5 parasaurolophus
6 triceratops
7 hypsilophodon
8 betasuchus
9 tyrannosaurus rex
10 pteranodon
11 gulls and waders

How intelligent were the dinosaurs?

Most people think of dinosaurs as large, stupid animals and it is probably true that the larger ones were not very intelligent. They had tiny brains in comparison to their size.

The giant dinosaurs like brachiosaurus and diplodocus were over 23 m (75 ft) long but they had very small heads by comparison and their brains were no bigger than a kitten's. Some dinosaurs were thought to have had a second brain above the back legs but this was not really a brain, only a nerve centre to control the rear part of the animal.

Even dinosaurs with larger heads were no more intelligent. The pachycephalosaurus had a skull 60 cm (2 ft) long and 22 cm (8½ ins) thick but the brain inside did not even fill the space for it. Many of the carnivorous dinosaurs (e.g. allosaurus) had huge heads but these housed a large jaw system which enabled the dinosaurs to swallow whole pieces of flesh. Their heads were full of teeth not brains!

The most intelligent dinosaurs were probably the fast-moving 'ostrich' dinosaurs and the flying pterosaurs. They had the largest brains in comparison to their body size. Their agility and strong eyesight, needed for hunting and flying, also indicate their intelligence.

Intelligent or not, the dinosaurs did 'rule' the world for 160 million years.

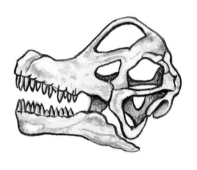

Brachiosaurus – head the size of a horse's but a brain no bigger than a kitten's.

Pachycephalosaurus – 'head bangers' had thick skulls but not much inside.

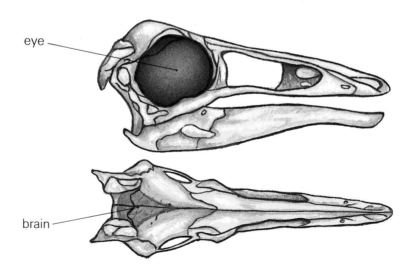

eye

brain

Dromiceiomimus – an 'ostrich' dinosaur with large eyes and a big brain.

Allosaurus – skull with rows of big, sharp teeth but not a very big brain.

Were they warm-blooded?

It is not known for certain whether dinosaurs were cold-blooded or warm-blooded. The reptiles of today are cold-blooded. This does not mean they have cold blood but that their body temperature varies with the air temperature. They rely on heat from the sun to warm their blood sufficiently to allow them to move freely. They shelter from the sun to cool down.

Birds and mammals, however, are warm-blooded. This means they maintain a constant body temperature. To achieve this, they eat more food when the weather is cold and when the weather is hot they lose heat by sweating or panting. Most warm-blooded animals have a covering of fur or feathers to help maintain their temperature.

There is a good case for thinking that the massive dinosaurs like brachiosaurus and diplodocus were cold-blooded. If they had been warm-blooded they would have had to spend all their time eating to maintain body temperature in such large bodies. It seems more likely that these slow movers were cold-blooded and gained heat by basking in the sun.

Another group of dinosaurs which probably used the sun to warm their blood were the spinosaurs. The **spinosaurus** had spines along its back that held a kind of sail of skin through which blood flowed. If it stood sideways to the sun at dawn (a) it could use its 'sail' as a 'solar panel' quickly warming its blood and making it active. When the sun became too hot at midday, the spinosaurus could lose heat by standing with its back to the sun (b).

On the other hand, many of the smaller dinosaurs like compsognathus, deinonychus and the 'ostrich' dinosaurs (e.g. **saurornithoides**) had erect postures, long limbs and were fast movers. As only warm-blooded creatures tend to move quickly, this suggests these animals were warm-blooded. Evidence also suggests that certain of these dinosaurs hunted at night, a time when cold-blooded creatures would be inactive.

a

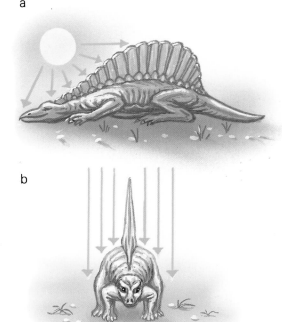

b

saurornithoides

Family Life

Fossil eggs, nests and young found recently tell us about how dinosaurs produced and raised their babies. When mating time drew near, males probably fought each other for females. First they threatened, then they banged heads or slashed with their clawed feet. Male dinosaurs with loud voices or large crests probably showed them off to attract their mates.

After mating, female dinosaurs laid eggs. Some females may have covered their eggs with sand and left them to hatch in the sun. Others built nests with raised mud rims and brooded their eggs as chickens do. It is possible that some females carried live young inside them, as many mammals do.

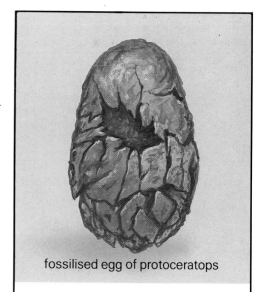

fossilised egg of protoceratops

A protoceratops' egg had ridges and wrinkles. When uncovered recently, the fossilised egg was red-brown.

Protoceratops laid eggs in hollows dug in sand. Each female laid a clutch of 12 or more, with the eggs' narrow ends facing inward. Very large clutches of eggs suggest that two females shared the nest.

The young protoceratops then hatched. Nearly all dinosaurs came from eggs. The eggs were warmed by the sun, mother's body or rotting leaves until they hatched.

The picture below shows a female **maiasaura** bringing food for her small hatchlings. She continued to feed her young until they could safely look for food on their own.

Certain dinosaurs bred in groups on hillsides. The adults shared the task of guarding the young. When old enough to look for their own food, these young dinosaurs were often protected in the herd by the adults. Many baby dinosaurs probably did not survive long enough to become fully developed. They were attacked and killed by carnivorous animals. Some adults killed their young if they were sick or wounded. However, a few dinosaurs may have lived for 100 years or more.

How big was a dinosaur egg? A baby hypselosaurus emerged from an egg 25 cm (10 ins) long and weighed approximately 1 kg (2.2 lb)..It grew to an adult length of 12 m (40 ft) and weighed 10 tonnes, 10,000 times its birthweight! Some adult dinosaurs were even bigger and heavier.

hen's egg and hypselosaurus egg shown to scale.

Little and large

The biggest dinosaurs were the largest animals that ever lived on land. Each had a huge, barrel-shaped body, four thick legs, a long neck with a small head and a very long tail. Despite their massive size, they were gentle giants. They ate leaves and plants.

Here you can see the tallest, the longest and the heaviest dinosaurs.

Not all dinosaurs were large – some were little. Indeed, some types of dinosaurs were smaller than you.

1 **Micropachycephalosaurus** was only 50 cm (20 ins) long. Its name means 'tiny thick-headed lizard'.

2 **Compsognathus** was smaller than a chicken. It was 60 cm (2 ft) long and weighed only 3 kg (6½ lb).

3 **Lesothosaurus** was about the size of a duck. It was about 90 cm (3 ft) long.

4 **Diplodocus** was the longest ever dinosaur. One set of fossil bones had a total length of 26.6 m (87½ ft). That is about the same length as 16 men and women laid end to end!

5 **Barosaurus** was probably the tallest. Although not as long overall as the diplodocus, this dinosaur had a very long neck. The longest of its neck bones was nearly 1 m (3 ft).

6 **Brachiosaurus** was the heaviest dinosaur. Adults weighed over 77 tonnes (85 tons). In 1979 American bone-hunters uncovered the fossilised remains of a monster. They gave it the nickname 'ultrasaurus'. Its weight was estimated to be the same as 30 large elephants.

39

Lizard-hips and bird-hips

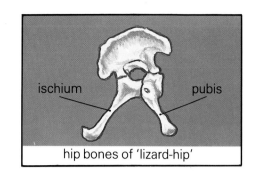

hip bones of 'lizard-hip'

In 1887 an English scientist named Henry Seeley introduced a new grouping among dinosaurs. He divided them into two orders, lizard-hips and bird-hips, according to the shape of their hip bones.

All animals need a framework of bone and muscle to support them as they move. Some dinosaurs had bones which were solid and heavy while others had hollow, light bones. The dinosaur's spine bore the strains and stresses of walking, running, feeding and fighting. The spine consists of bones or segments known as vertebrae. The number of these varied depending on the dinosaur's size and shape. As a rule, the hind legs were larger and stronger than the forelimbs ('arms'). The main weight of the body rested on the hind legs and was supported by the hip bones. It is the shape of this hip girdle which places dinosaurs into one of the two groups.

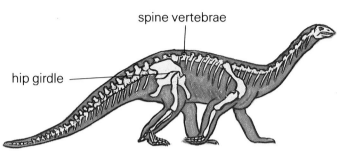

partial skeleton of 'lizard-hip'

'Lizard-hips' had a hip girdle arranged like those of lizards, crocodiles and other reptiles. The largest and fiercest dinosaurs belonged to this group. The four-legged giants barosaurus and brachiosaurus were 'lizard-hip' dinosaurs as were all the two-legged carnivores, such as **tyrannosaurus** (1) and megalosaurus.

Plateosaurus (2) walked on all fours but probably reared up to eat leaves high up, using its 'arms' as a prop.

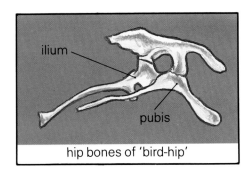

hip bones of 'bird-hip'

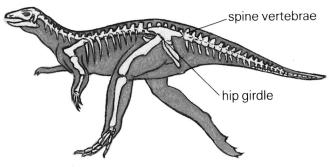

partial skeleton of 'bird-hip'

spine vertebrae

hip girdle

ilium

pubis

The second order of dinosaurs is known as the 'bird-hips'. This is because their hip bones are arranged in the same way as those of a bird. Look at the drawings of the two types of hip girdle (above and on opposite page) to see the difference.

'Bird-hip' dinosaurs did not evolve until some way into the Jurassic Period. There was a wide range of species among the 'bird-hips'. Some walked on two legs, such as the **hypsilophodon** (3) and **fabrosaurus** (4). Others walked on all fours. Stegosaurus and ankylosaurus lumbered along, feeding on low-lying plants. 'Bird-hip' dinosaurs had an extra bone forming a tip to the lower jaw. Many had a horny beak, strong teeth and cheek pouches. All of them were herbivores.

Fabrosaurus was one of the first 'bird-hips'. This small animal was about 1 m (3¼ ft) long. Hypsilophodon was a fast runner, using its great speed to avoid predators.

Plant-eating dinosaurs

Some dinosaurs developed large hind legs and short front legs. They used their back legs for running and their front legs for grasping food.

Most dinosaurs were herbivores (plant-eaters). They had teeth shaped like pegs. When these wore down, new teeth grew in their place. **Anatosaurus** (1) had more than 1000 teeth in its wide jaws. It was a duck-billed dinosaur. Some plant-eating dinosaurs devloped into huge animals – the largest ever to live on land. **Diplodocus** (2) was the longest dinosaur. It was 26.6 m (87½ ft) long.

Plant-eating dinosaurs probably had a keen sense of smell. This helped them to know when predators were near. Some ran away. Others, like diplodocus, would lash

out with their tails. If that failed to scare off the attacker, the dinosaur would rear up and crash down its front legs (as an elephant does to crush a tiger). Other dinosaurs had horny plates and spikes. **Triceratops** (3) had three horns. At 9 m (30 ft) from beak to tip of tail, it was one of the largest horned dinosaurs. When a triceratops put its head down and charged, predators probably ran away.

Herds of bonehead dinosaurs also roamed the plains eating the vegetation. Two adult male **stegoceras** (4) charged towards each other and banged their heads together. The winner of the duel probably ruled the herd of females. These boneheads had a brain the size of a hen's eggs inside a bony dome five times thicker than the skull of a human.

Meat-eating dinosaurs

Most carnivores in the dinosaur world walked and ran on their hind legs. Many of these speedy runners had a stiffened tail. This helped them to balance on their strong hind legs. Some carnivores were no bigger than a chicken. Only the larger meat-eaters were a real threat to the plant-eating dinosaurs.

The dinosaur chasing a lizard is a **compsognathus** (1). We know this carnivore caught such prey because its fossilised rib-cage has been found containing lizard bones. Smaller than a chicken, it was 60 cm (2 ft) long and weighed only 4 kg (6½ lb). Compsognathus was possibly the ancestor of birds (see page 61).

Tyrannosaurus rex (2) was king of the carnivores. It was 12 m (39 ft) from nose to tail. It was probably not a fast runner. Tyrannosaurus tended to feed on dead or injured dinosaurs. If it caught live prey, its teeth might have snapped off during the fight. The sharp claws on its hind feet were

used as carving knives and it tore off lumps of flesh with its fangs. Strangely, its tiny arms were too weak to use as weapons and too short to lift food to its mouth.

The name **deinonychus** (3) means 'terrible claw'. This ferocious carnivore had the first toe turned back and the second toe had a claw 12.5 cm (5 inches) long. When it caught up with its prey, deinonychus would leap up, lashing out with its claws and pin it to the ground.

This meat-eater was 3 m (10 ft) long.

The 8 m (26 ft) long herbivore, **stegosaurus** (4) would have been preyed on by the 10 m (32½ft) long **allosaurus** (5). Its plates made the stegosaurus look bigger than it actually was and the allosaurus was nimble enough to dodge the spikes on the stegosaurus' tail. The allosaurus had razor-sharp teeth and large claws. Its huge jaws could gape wide enough for it to shove great chunks of meat inside.

Plates, spikes and horns

Those land-living dinosaurs unable to escape the speedy carnivores needed some form of protection. Some developed bony plates, while others sprouted horns or frills.

In the Jurassic Period, **stegosaurus** had two rows of pointed, bony plates along its back from neck to tail. The largest of these was 75 cm (2½ ft) high and about the same across. These may have served as a form of body heating, drawing heat from the sun, but they also made the stegosaurus look bigger. On its tail were at least four heavy spikes. Its back legs were twice as high as its front legs. Plated dinosaurs like stegosaurus died out because a carnivore's claws and fangs could pierce the areas of skin unprotected by plates.

In the Cretaceous Period, creatures known as 'reptilian tanks' replaced the plated dinosaurs. Tough skin covered flexible bony slabs and spikes, protecting all the upper parts of the beast's body. **Ankylosaurus** was the largest of these spiky dinosaurs. When attacked, it probably drew its head in and got as close to the ground as it could, to protect its soft underside from attack – as the armadillo does today. Its bony tail club made a useful weapon. Spiky dinosaurs had small teeth and weak jaws. They fed on soft plants and insects.

The horned dinosaurs evolved later in the Cretaceous Period. Although they looked fearsome, these plant-eaters were harmless unless provoked. Some were covered in horns and spikes, others had very long frills. They ranged from creatures lighter than an adult human to monsters twice as long as a rhinoceros and as heavy as a large elephant. Their ancestor was probably the **psittacosaurus** (1). This 'parrot lizard' had short bony plates jutting back from the sides of the head.

The **styracosaurus** (2) had one straight nose horn and six long spikes jutting backward from the skull. The spikes were an adaptation of the bony neck frill of the **triceratops** (3). Measuring 9 m (30 ft) from beak to tip of tail, the triceratops was one of the largest and one of the last of the horned dinosaurs. Two horns, each 1 m (3¼ ft) long, grew from its forehead and a third was seated on the nose. The back of its skull spread out to form a bony collar which protected the dinosaur's neck when its head was raised. When a determined triceratops put its head down and charged, even the tyrannosaurus probably ran away!

Horned dinosaurs probably lived in herds, and it is likely that the adults protected the young from attackers by forming an outward-facing ring. This would have stopped any predator from getting too close. The horned dinosaurs would have used their horns as defence weapons.

Head-bangers

'Boneheads' were two-footed dinosaurs with thick skulls. They may have evolved from the same ancestor as horned dinosaurs, the psittacosaurus. Herds of 'boneheads' roamed hills in North America and Asia in the Cretaceous Period. Each herd had a strong male as its leader. Many munched leaves, seeds, fruit and possibly insects.

Male 'boneheads' had thicker skulls than females. The roof of the skull was expanded to form a dome. **Stegoceras** had a brain the size of a hen's egg. Yet that brain was inside a bony dome five times thicker than your skull.

The biggest 'bonehead' of them all was **pachycephalosaurus** whose skull was 22 cm (8½ ins) thick. That is 20 times thicker than a human skull. Bony spikes jutted upwards from above the snout and bony knobs rimmed the back of the head.

Why did 'boneheads' have such thick skulls? The answer may be that males would fight over the females or to decide who would lead the herd. Crash! They banged their heads together. Probably they did not fight to kill. 'Boneheads' may also have used their thick skulls to drive away predators.

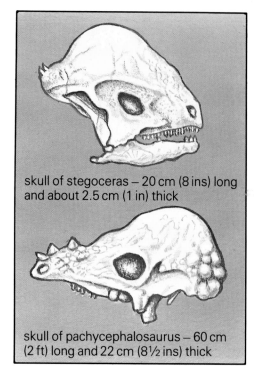

skull of stegoceras – 20 cm (8 ins) long and about 2.5 cm (1 in) thick

skull of pachycephalosaurus – 60 cm (2 ft) long and 22 cm (8½ ins) thick

When two male stegoceras crashed head-on, there was no damage to the brain or backbone because the thick bone acted as a pad to absorb the blow.

Duck-billed dinosaurs

As 'boneheads' roamed hills, a strange relative browsed among conifer trees in northern lands. These dinosaurs walked on three-toed hind legs and used their long, heavy tail as a prop when resting or feeding. Both arms had four webbed fingers.

Duckbills got their name from their toothless beaks. At the back of the mouth, however, were hundreds of teeth designed to grind tough leaves. **Anatosaurus** had about 1000 teeth in its wide jaws. It was one of the largest duckbills – up to 13 m (42½ ft) long. Loose skin on its flat face could be blown up to help it make a loud bellowing call.

anatosaurus

① ② ③ ④ ⑤ ⑥

Some duck-billed dinosaurs had a crest on top of the head. Different kinds had different crests. **Saurolophus** (1) had a spiky crest and a frill at the back of its skull. It may have been able to blow up skin balloons along the length of its face. **Parasaurolophus** (2) had a 1.8 m (6 ft) horn curving backward from the top of its head. **Corythosaurus** (3) had a tall, rounded crest like a helmet.

Why did these duck-billed dinosaurs have a crest? It was not for head-banging. It was simply to help them recognise their own kind. The **lambeosaurus** males (4) had larger crests than the females (5) and their young (6). At mating time the head crests, bellowing calls or skin flaps blown up like balloons, probably helped males and females of the same species to find each other.

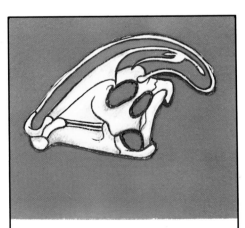

Diagram of skull of a female parasaurolophus. When these duck-billed dinosaurs called to one another their long air passages (in red) made a sound like a bugle or hunting horn.

Strange beasts

'Ostrich' dinosaurs

These strange beasts lived late in the Age of Dinosaurs. They looked something like ostriches without feathers, with their long necks and long legs. They used their arms to gather fruits and to tear open ants' nests. When they walked or ran, they held their tail out stiffly level with their back. These dinosaurs had good eyesight. If an enemy came near, they ran away quickly.

'Ostrich' dinosaurs had light, hollow bones. They were around 3.5 m (11½ ft) in length. More than half the length of **ornithomimus** was its tail. This strange beast lived in forests and swamps in North America, feeding on lizards and mammals, insects and fruit, and sometimes eggs.

ornithomimus

Oviraptor was also an 'ostrich' dinosaur but was known as the 'egg thief'. It had a toothless beak and strong jaws. It used its lower jaw to crush hard food, such as tough egg shells.

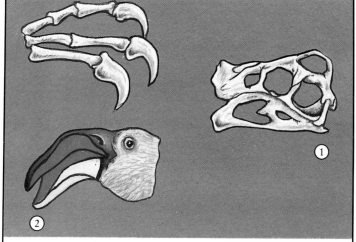

The egg thief's fingers had long bones and strong, curved claws. The first finger claw is about 8 cm (3 ins) long.

Oviraptor had a short, deep skull (1). It looks like no other known dinosaur's, yet it is similar in shape to the head of a flamingo (2).

Feathered dinosaur

Archaeopteryx looked like a cross between a bird and a reptile. It was about the size of a crow and had feathered wings. It had a toe which pointed backward on each foot, like today's birds. It probably could not fly far but it was a fast runner, possibly quick enough to catch flying insects. Like reptiles, this strange beast's jaws were lined with tiny teeth. Three clawed fingers sprouted from each 'feathered arm'.

archaeopteryx

Baby hippo?

Lystrosaurus was a mammal-like reptile. It led a life similar to that of the modern hippopotamus. It wallowed in mud, eating water plants. It was small – only about 80 cm (2½ ft). To build a den it scraped a hole with its powerful front legs. A single pair of fangs stuck out from its snout. Fossil bones were found in southern Africa and the Antarctic. This suggests that these two continents were joined together in the Triassic Period (see picture of Earth – page 28).

lystrosaurus

mastodonsaurus

Giant frog?

Mastodonsaurus lived all its life under water. It looked like a huge frog and was over 3 m (10 ft) long. Its jaws were armed with sharp teeth. Short legs and a short tail show that this beast preferred swimming to walking.

Monsters of the deep

The largest dinosaurs were so huge that they could not move very well on land. Their enormous body and neck was supported by four short legs. Imagine carrying round a load weighing 77 tonnes (85 tons)! **Brachiosaurus** spent most of its time in water which helped to support its tremendous body weight. It could not swim so it would walk slowly out from the bank or shore up to shoulder height. The brachiosaurus was safe from predators while it stayed in the water. There were plenty of water plants to eat. It was probably content to stand for hours in the water. It is a curious feature of the brachiosaurus that its nostrils were on top of its head. It was thought at one time that the brachiosaurus would breathe through them when in deep water but it is now known that the pressure of the water at that depth would have been too great. It would have crushed its lungs and killed it.

During the Age of Dinosaurs large reptiles could be found in the oceans as well as on the land. Plesiosaurs ('near lizard') were big sea creatures with short tails which were not much use for swimming. Instead they rowed using their broad, flat flippers. Some had long necks, others had short necks.

The long-necked type swam on the surface with its small head held above the water. It could flex its neck like the body of a snake. **Elasmosaurus** (1) was the largest known plesiosaur. About half of its 14 m (47 ft) length was its head and neck. The strange thing about this long-necked creature was that it was unable to dive down. This was because it could not lift its four flippers higher than the shoulders and hips. When it saw a fish, it would stab down on its prey with its head.

The short-necked type had a large head with powerful jaws. In its huge mouth were dagger-like teeth. It could swim faster and farther than the long-necked creatures. To hunt for food it dived down to the deep. **Kronosaurus** (2) was 12 m (39 ft) long. Its head alone was longer than two men lying end to end.

53

Monsters in the air

By the Cretaceous Period there were not only monster dinosaurs roaming the land and fierce reptiles in the seas, there were also creatures in the air. They were not true birds. In fact, they evolved from the same group of reptiles that led to dinosaurs. They may have come from a small, tree-dwelling animal known as **podopteryx**. A web of skin linked the fore and hind limbs and the hind limbs with the base of the tail. Podopteryx used this skin to glide like present-day flying lizards and flying squirrels.

podopteryx

rhamphorhynchus in the air

The (pterosaurs) 'winged lizards' that evolved had a skeleton of thin, hollow bones. Each skin wing was fixed to the long bones of the arm and curved back to the hind legs. The muscles of many pterosaurs were too weak to flap their wings. They simply glided on currents of warm air. They swooped low to seize fish and small lizards. The long beak-like jaw was full of teeth.

Pterosaurs were clumsy on land because their legs were very short. They could only shuffle along. They probably hung upside down on cliffs or treetops to sleep – like bats. Here they were safe from enemies.

There were two main groups of pterosaurs. One group, the 'prow-beaks', used their long tail like a rudder. **Rhamphorhynchus** had a body only 45 cm (1½ ft) long. That is about the size of an eagle.

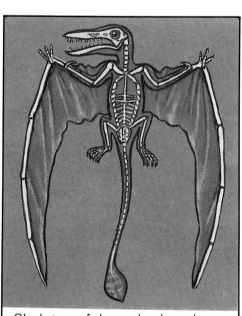

Skeleton of rhamphorhynchus – with wings attached to the extra long fourth finger of each hand.

The second group of pterosaurs were the pterodactyls. This name means 'winged fingers'. These creatures had long wings, little or no tail and a toothless beak. Some were as small as a sparrow, some were many times larger than an eagle.

Pteranodon was a pterodactyl with a wingspan of 7.6 m (25 ft). A fully-grown adult weighed 18 kg (40 lb). The skull of this flying reptile extended back into a long bony crest. This may have been used as a rudder to help it steer (instead of a tail) or to counterbalance the weight of the beak. From fossilised remains that have been found, scientists believe that the pteranodon flew as far as 100 km (62 miles) out over the sea. It scooped up fish in its long beak. Here is an adult pteranodon dropping fish from its mouth pouch to its young.

Quetzalcoatlus had a wingspan of over 12 m (39 ft), from tip to tip. This makes it the largest creature ever to have flown on Earth. No one knows how such a huge beast got up into the air. In 1975 fossil bones of this reptile were found in Texas, USA. As they were found inland it is possible that quetzalcoatlus was a kind of reptilian vulture that fed on dead animals.

Why did dinosaurs die out?

About 65 million years ago dinosaurs vanished from the face of the Earth. This may have taken anything from a few years to five million years. Experts cannot agree on this. Why did this happen to a group of animals that had ruled so successfully for so long? It was not only the land-living dinosaurs that died out but also the monsters in the air and the monsters of the deep. Many other land and sea creatures also died out. However, snakes, lizards, crocodiles, frogs, toads, salamanders, birds and some mammals survived.

Many theories have been suggested. Here are some of them. None of these theories has been proved correct.

Was it a natural disaster such as a flood, earthquake or volcano eruption? This is unlikely because all forms of life would have been affected.

Egg thieves may have stolen all the eggs so that no young were born.

Perhaps carnivores ate all the plant-eaters and then ate each other.

Did the dinosaurs grow so large that they could not breed or move?

Did new flowering plants poison them?

Did a plague of caterpillars strip the leaves from trees?

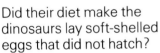

Did their diet make the dinosaurs lay soft-shelled eggs that did not hatch?

A rock – 10 km (6 miles) across – may have streaked from space and hit the Earth. The impact could have hurled dust and moisture up into the atmosphere, darkening the sky for months and killing all the vegetation.

The theory that makes the most sense is the one that suggests there was a sudden and dramatic change of climate. The theory is that winters became very much colder. If dinosaurs were warm-blooded, they lacked fur or feathers to trap their body heat. If they were cold-blooded, many dinosaurs were too big to hibernate in frost-free holes. The cold would have killed many plants leaving less food for plant-eating dinosaurs. If these died from starvation, there would have been fewer dinosaurs for the flesh-eaters to prey on and they too would starve to death. A similar fate would have been in store for the monsters in the seas. Flying monsters would have suffered too. A drop in temperature at the poles would have led to an increase in wind strengths and speeds. These creatures were gliders, not flappers. They would have lost control in stronger winds and crashed to the ground.

The vanishing dinosaurs remains one of the great mysteries. Whatever the reason, it is sad that these exciting and fascinating creatures who ruled for 160 million years had to die out. When the Age of Dinosaurs ended, the Age of Mammals began.

Digging up a dinosaur

How do fossil hunters find the remains of dinosaurs? In the early years of fossil hunting many finds were made by accident. Now the experts know the most likely places. It is rare for bones to be lying around ready to be put straight into a bag or box. They are often found in cliffs and quarries. New dinosaurs are still being found and a recent find in a Surrey clay pit in 1983 has been named baryonyx walkeri ('heavy clawed creature found by Mr Walker'). This unique carnivorous dinosaur species had 128 teeth instead of the usual 64, and is believed to have preyed on fish.

When fossil remains are found, notes are made of where they were found. Then begins the task of removing the fossils. The soil and rock are removed until half the bone is exposed (1). Foil or wet tissue paper is wrapped round the bone (2). Then foam or plaster of Paris is added. This hardens to form a protective casing (3). Next they dig away the surrounding soil, turn the bone over and wrap the other half. Small fossils are placed in bags and large ones in crates (4).

The fossils are then cleaned. This may take years. First scientists soak, saw or slice away the foam or plaster bandages. Weak areas of exposed bone are hardened with special chemicals. Hard rock is chipped away with hammer and chisel. A dentist's drill is often used to speed up the work.

Scientists then rebuild the skeleton of the dinosaur, with missing pieces rebuilt in glass fibre.

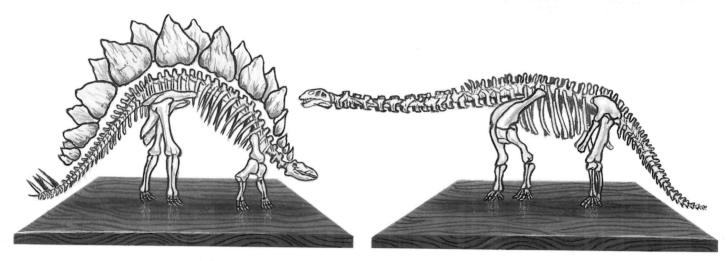

stegosaurus skeleton

apatosaurus skeleton

In the museum

Natural history museums often produce life-size copies of dinosaur skeletons. They make plaster moulds of the bones and fill these with glass fibre to form casts. The skeleton of one of the giant dinosaurs often fills an entire hall in a museum. Whole scenes showing dinosaurs and landscapes are recreated as realistically as possible to help you understand more about the exciting creatures that lived on the Earth so many millions of years ago.

allosaurus skeleton

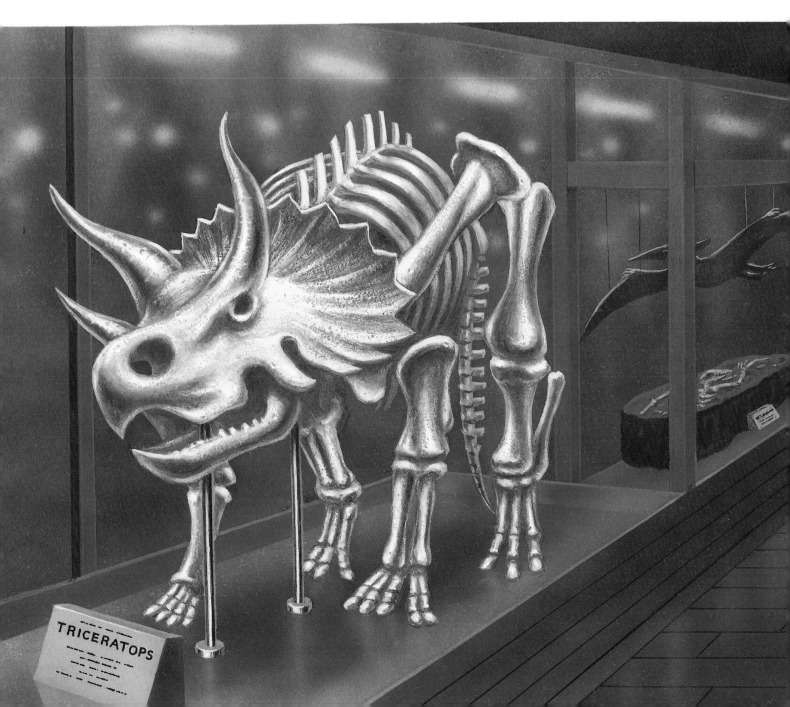

TRICERATOPS

New Life

65 million–5,000 years ago

All dinosaurs and most reptiles vanished from the face of the Earth around 65 million years ago. Why did this happen? Perhaps there were natural disasters such as floods or earthquakes. Perhaps carnivores ate all the herbivores and then ate each other. It was more probably caused by a change in the climate that made it too cold for the dinosaurs and they could not adapt. Whatever the cause, the death of the dinosaurs signalled the start of the New Life, the Age of Mammals.

During this period, mammals evolved shapes and sizes that suited them for life in almost all places. Some took to the air (1), others went into water. The first hoofed herbivores (2) and the first rodents (3) appeared. As grasses grew, so grazing mammals evolved – beasts that looked like horses (4), camels (5) and rhinos (6).

Large flightless birds (7) began to evolve in the places where there were no big reptiles or mammals that could prey on them. Some birds (8) took to hunting prey at night. **Ichthyornis** (9) was the first known bird with a breastbone designed to support the muscles needed for flying. The **long-legged wader** (10) was the ancestor of ducks and geese.

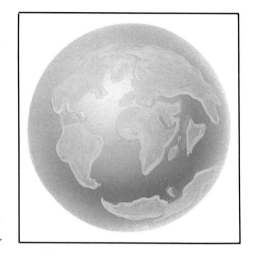

Earth – 40 million years ago
As land masses moved apart, climates cooled. Different types of mammals developed in different lands.

Key

1 bats
2 uintatherium
3 paramys
4 hyracotherium
5 alticamelus
6 arsinoitherium
7 diatryma
8 ogygoptynx
9 ichthyornis
10 proardea

Birds

The prehistoric animal which links birds to their dinosaur ancestors was probably **archaeopteryx**. It had solid bones like a reptile, yet it had feathered wings like a bird. Three clawed fingers sprouted from each 'feathered arm'. Archaeopteryx was too big to fly and it was not a good glider as its wings were too short. It was probably a fast runner, able to catch flying insects.

Hesperornis, an early true bird, had very small wings. It was clumsy on land, using its tail to help it balance. Its webbed feet were used for swimming. Hesperornis seized fish in its toothed jaws.

A large flightless bird stalked the plains of North America 50 million years ago. Taller than an adult human, **diatryma** had a huge beak which made it look fierce. Its body and small wings were covered in fine feathers.

archaeopteryx

hesperornis

Although these birds died out millions of years ago, there are still large flightless birds alive today. The most famous are the **ostrich**, emu and cassowary.

diatryma

Mammals

Not all reptiles could adapt to the new colder conditions. However, mammals had evolved with the ability to keep their bodies warm at all times. This was helped by the body covering of hair. Being warm-blooded allowed some mammals to carry on hunting prey at night. They also looked after their young.

Only fossil teeth and jaws have been found of these early mammals. The first mammals were insect-eating shrews, like **megazostrodon**.

We know about early mammals from looking at the primitive mammals that are alive today. The **echidna** is a spiny anteater. It has no ears and has little control over its body temperature. A female echidna places leathery eggs at the bottom of a closed burrow and keeps them warm for two weeks. The tiny young then attach themselves to hairs in the mother's pouch.

The largest known land mammal that ever lived was the **indricotherium** which was 5.5 m (18 ft) tall at the shoulder. This giant, hornless, rhinoceros-like animal died out some 20 million years ago. Its great size enabled the indricotherium to feed on leaves at the tops of trees.

The most successful mammals in terms of numbers and variety are the rodents. This group includes rats, squirrels, beavers, porcupines and many more. Rodents live in trees, on mountains, under the ground and in streams. The first known rodent was **paramys** (1). It was a climber like a squirrel.

Possibly the largest flesh-eating mammal ever was **megistotherium** (2). Its head was twice as big as any bear's. This monster weighed about 900 kg (1980 lb).

Uintatherium was a hoofed animal and stood 2 m (6½ ft) at the shoulder. This slow-moving plant-eater lived in North America.

It had three pairs of horny swellings on top of its skull. Males also had a pair of tusks that rested on another bony outgrowth.

Mammals rule

By 35 million years ago large flesh-eating mammals ruled most continents. They had bigger brains, keener ears and were faster than other mammals. In the picture below, a very big cat, **smilodon** (1) is on top of a large prehistoric herbivore, **megatherium** (2). Smilodon was an American 'sabre-tooth tiger'. It used strong neck muscles to stab its teeth into prey. Megatherium was a huge ground sloth, 6 m (20 ft) long and nearly twice as tall as an adult human. It walked on its knuckles and the sides of its feet. When it reared up, its strong tail acted as a prop. Then it could claw leaves into its mouth. Megatherium probably died out after humans invaded the forests where they lived. It is possible that sabre-tooth tigers caught and killed creatures as large as the **mastodon** (3). This prehistoric elephant had a furry coat of red hair.

Around 20 million years ago there were many animals in North America. Those shown here all have hoofed feet and chew their food. **Alticamelus** (1) was a prehistoric camel-giraffe. If it lifted its head it could feed on leafy twigs 3 m (10 ft) off the ground. **Synthetoceras** (2) was a prehistoric type of deer. Males grew Y-shaped horns jutting up from the nose and a pair of shorter horns behind the eyes. **Brontotherium** (3) was between a rhinoceros and an elephant in size. It had three hoofed toes on each hind foot and four toes on each front foot. Males probably used their horns when fighting.

More mammals

The first known horse was about the size of a fox. **Hyracotherium** or 'dawn horse' was only 40 cm (1¼ ft) tall at the shoulder. It munched soft leaves 50 million years ago in swampy North American and European forests before the continents finally separated. Its descendants died out in Europe but continued to evolve in North America. Later stages crossed back into Europe and continued their evolution, but the horse mysteriously died out in America. The modern horse, **equus**, evolved about 2 million years ago. It spread into most continents but was reintroduced into America only a few hundred years ago by man. Wild species alive today include Przewalski's horse of Mongolia, the wild ass and the zebra.

Certain mammals returned to a life in water. **Basilosaurus** (1) was an early whale – up to 20 m (66 ft) long. It had saw-edged teeth. Its front limbs were flippers and there were no hind limbs. The early relative of sea-lions was **allodesmus** (2). It looked like the largest seal alive today, the sea-elephant.

The **cave bear** was a large member of the dog family. At about 4 m (13 ft) tall on its hind feet, it was well over a third larger than even the biggest of the modern brown bears. Rounded teeth indicate that the cave bear fed mainly on plants. Its home was often in the mountains of Europe.

The **mammoth** (1) and the **woolly rhinoceros** (2) lived on the icy tundra within sight of the great ice sheets during the ice ages in Europe and North America. They both had long hair and thick underfur. The woolly mammoth used its tusks to defend itself and possibly to clear snow off plant food. The woolly rhino was able to dig up roots with its large horn. There is evidence that mammoths also lived in other continents. Cave paintings show mammoths being hunted by early cave-people. Mammoths died out about 10,000 years ago. The modern Indian elephant is the closest living relative to the mammoths.

The arrival of mankind

About 65 million years ago, a group of shrew-like animals began to live in the trees. This may have been to escape predators. These animals evolved into the first example of a primate 20 million years ago, called **prosimian** (1) – the ancestor of humans as well as apes and monkeys.

From prosimian came two branches, one was **ramapithecus** (2), the ancestor of mankind and the other was dryopithecus, the ancestor of monkeys and chimpanzees. The chimpanzee is therefore our 'cousin' and probably our closest relative in the animal kingdom.

Ramapithecus looked more like an ape than a man and lived about 10 million years ago. Its skeleton structure shows that after several million years it was walking upright and therefore probably using its hands to pick roots and fruits or to hold a stick or stone as a weapon.

Between 4 million and 1½ million years ago, **australopithecus** (3) evolved. It was definitely more human-like. It lived in groups and was starting to eat meat as well as vegetation. It therefore had to find better ways to kill. It was not big, up to 1.2 m (4 ft) tall, nor very strong, so it had to invent weapons and learn to hunt small animals. It probably used old bones as clubs.

About 2 million years ago, the first human being appeared. His skeleton was very close to ours. He was called **homo habilis** (handy man) (4). He made stone weapons and tools. He began to make very primitive shelters. He was about 1.3 m

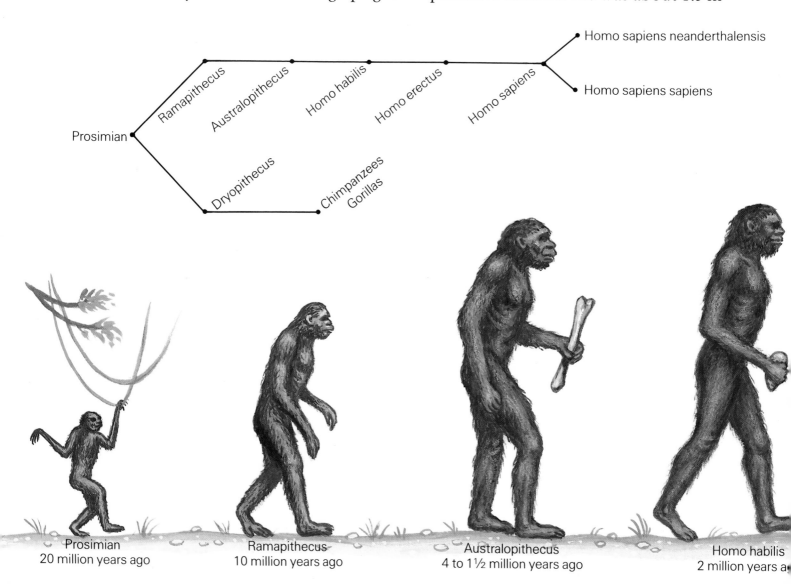

Prosimian
20 million years ago

Ramapithecus
10 million years ago

Australopithecus
4 to 1½ million years ago

Homo habilis
2 million years a[...]

(4¼ ft) tall. His successor was **homo erectus** (upright man) (5), who appeared between 1 million and 800,000 years ago. He was continually improving stone tools, mainly by putting handles on them. He was taller and stronger than homo habilis. His body and limbs were very similar to ours, but the skull was still changing. As he became more intelligent, homo erectus used his hands more and made tools to do what his jaws had done before. Over a long period, his jaws became smaller making him look more like a modern man. His greatest discovery was fire about 400,000 years ago. In China, a fireplace was found with a pile of ashes that were 6 m (19½ ft) deep, showing that the fire had been kept continually burning for many generations.

Homo erectus gradually evolved into **homo sapiens** (wise man) (6) and for a long time groups of both types of primitive human beings lived alongside each other until homo erectus died out leaving homo sapiens. One form of homo sapiens, **Neanderthal man** (7), appeared about 150,000 to 100,000 years ago and died out about 35,000 years ago. He was about 1.6 m (5 ft) tall.

About 45,000 years ago, the last link appeared. This was **homo sapiens sapiens** (8) who was probably responsible for the extinction of Neanderthal man. He was physically no different from humans today. From then on as his intelligence increased, he travelled further, built homes and eventually, 5,000 years ago, began recording his activities in ancient writing.

Homo erectus
1 million years ago

Homo sapiens
800,000 years ago

Homo sapiens neanderthalensis
150,000 years ago

Homo sapiens sapiens
45,000 years ago

Neanderthal man

The best-known primitive human is Neanderthal man. He lived from about 150,000 to 35,000 years ago.

He was similar in build to us but a little shorter and stockier. His face was broad, with a heavy brow over his eyes and no chin. He probably had a very basic language. He lived in a group probably made up of several families. Each winter they would return to a permanent winter home after following the herds of mammoth and woolly rhinoceroses all summer. Neanderthal man was a skilful hunter, using spears and clubs to bring down these big animals. He wore skins to keep warm in the cold conditions near the ice sheets where he lived during the Ice Age.

Fire was used for protection as well as for warmth. A fire in an entrance to a cave would deter most animals. They also used it for cooking and for hardening wooden spears.

They buried their dead, often with tools and flowers. Sometimes bones of an ibex, cave bear or lion were buried with them, suggesting that these animals may have been sacred to Neanderthal man.

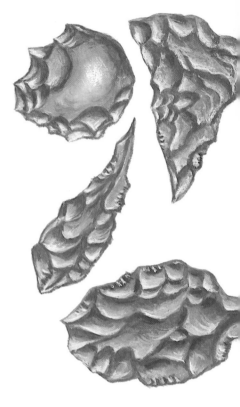

Primitive people were quite skilled at making stone tools and weapons of various sizes. Hand-axes, scrapers, knives, spikes and drills were chipped out of stone.

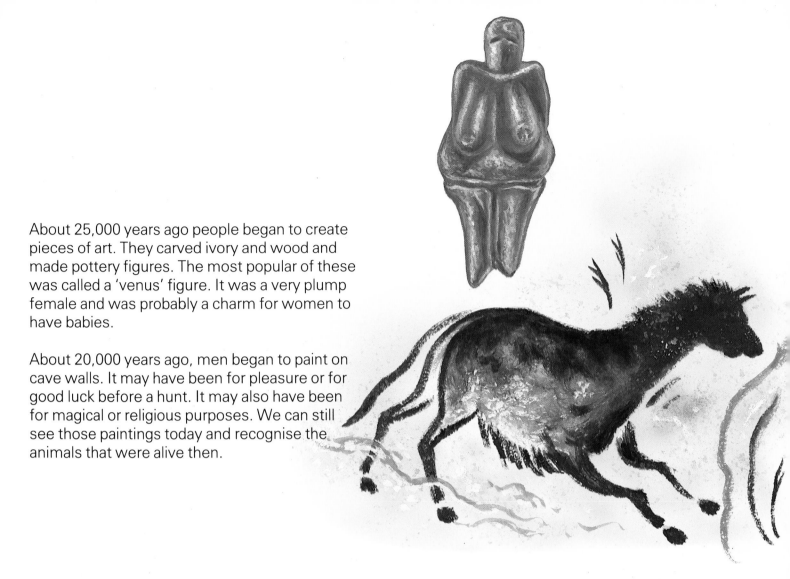

About 25,000 years ago people began to create pieces of art. They carved ivory and wood and made pottery figures. The most popular of these was called a 'venus' figure. It was a very plump female and was probably a charm for women to have babies.

About 20,000 years ago, men began to paint on cave walls. It may have been for pleasure or for good luck before a hunt. It may also have been for magical or religious purposes. We can still see those paintings today and recognise the animals that were alive then.

Fossils

When animals die their bodies rot, often leaving no trace. But, if conditions are right, some parts may be preserved. An animal may have died and been buried in a seabed, a riverbed, a desert or even under snow. Layers of mud, sand or ice would have built up over the years burying the remains deep below ground. The hard parts of the animals may be preserved in the rock as fossils; some animals could even be preserved whole in ice. Slow wearing away of rock or sudden earth movements such as earthquakes can expose the deep layers and reveal those fossils that have been hidden for thousands or millions of years. By studying these remains, scientists are able to trace the history of life on earth and the links between the ancient and modern animal species.

Traces of the earliest forms of life have been found in Australia. Fossilised layers of limestone created by **blue-green algae** date back 3,500 million years. Embedded in sandstone, also in Australia, the remains of 600 million year old **jellyfish** have been found.

Fish fossils have been found dating back as far as about 430 million years ago. An amazing find at the site of an ancient lake in Italy revealed over 100,000 fossilised **fish**; the earliest of them were dated as 55 million years old. They lived in a lake overshadowed by a volcano. Each time the volcano erupted, the fish in the lake were 'cooked' and their remains buried. This left several layers of fossilised fish.

Insects are extremely frail and therefore do not often preserve as fossils, except under the most ideal conditions (being covered with a layer of mud that dries hard). Some insect finds on land have been traced back to about 345 million years ago, but the best finds are of insects trapped in tree resin (sap) which has hardened to form amber. The best fossil **insects in amber** were found by the Baltic Sea and are about 30 million years old.

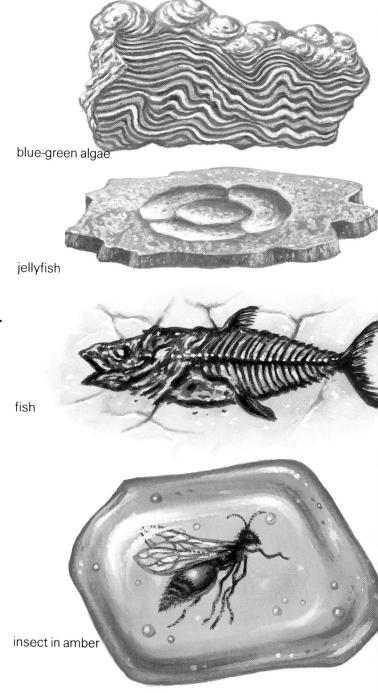

blue-green algae

jellyfish

fish

insect in amber

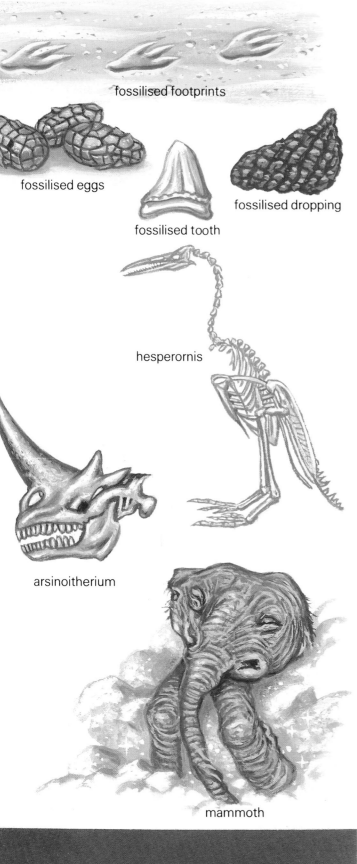

fossilised footprints

fossilised eggs

fossilised tooth

fossilised dropping

hesperornis

arsinoitherium

mammoth

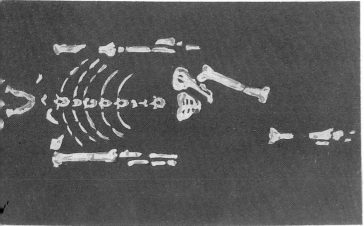

The age of the reptiles, particularly that of the dinosaurs, has been a rich source of fossil finds. From these, scientists can build up a full picture of what the dinosaurs were like. The spacing of **fossilised footprints** tells them how fast they moved; bones tell them how big the dinosaurs were. **Fossilised eggs**, some with babies still inside, supply information about their breeding habits; **fossilised teeth** and **droppings** give clues to what the dinosaurs ate. The skeletons of 31 iguanodon found together in a Belgian coal mine support the view that some herbivores probably roamed in herds.

Like insects, bird fossils are rare because of the frailty of the bones, but the earliest true birds have been dated at about 80 million years old. One was **hesperornis**, for which all the bones have been found and pieced together.

Fossils from the age of mammals have provided evidence of animals which are now extinct and also of the ancestors of some modern day animals. The double-horned **arsinoitherium**, which has no living descendant, has been found in Egypt and dated as 37 million years old. **Mammoths** and woolly rhinoceroses, ancestors of the Indian elephant and rhinoceros, have been found deep-frozen in Siberia.

Evidence of our own primitive ancestors has also been found. This can be traced back about 60 million years to a shrew-like tree-living primate. **'Lucy'** (left) found in Africa, is the most complete australopithecus skeleton ever found. This has been dated as 3½ million years old. It clearly shows the link between humans and our ape-like ancestors.

Index

The numbers in circles refer to the map of the world as it is today (page 78–79). The numbers that follow are page references. In the case of the dinosaurs, a translation of the name is given in italic, followed by a short description of the animal

The circled numbers show where fossils of each dinosaur have been found. The dinosaur silhouettes around the map are not drawn to scale, however we have tried to show some difference in size between the larger and smaller dinosaurs.

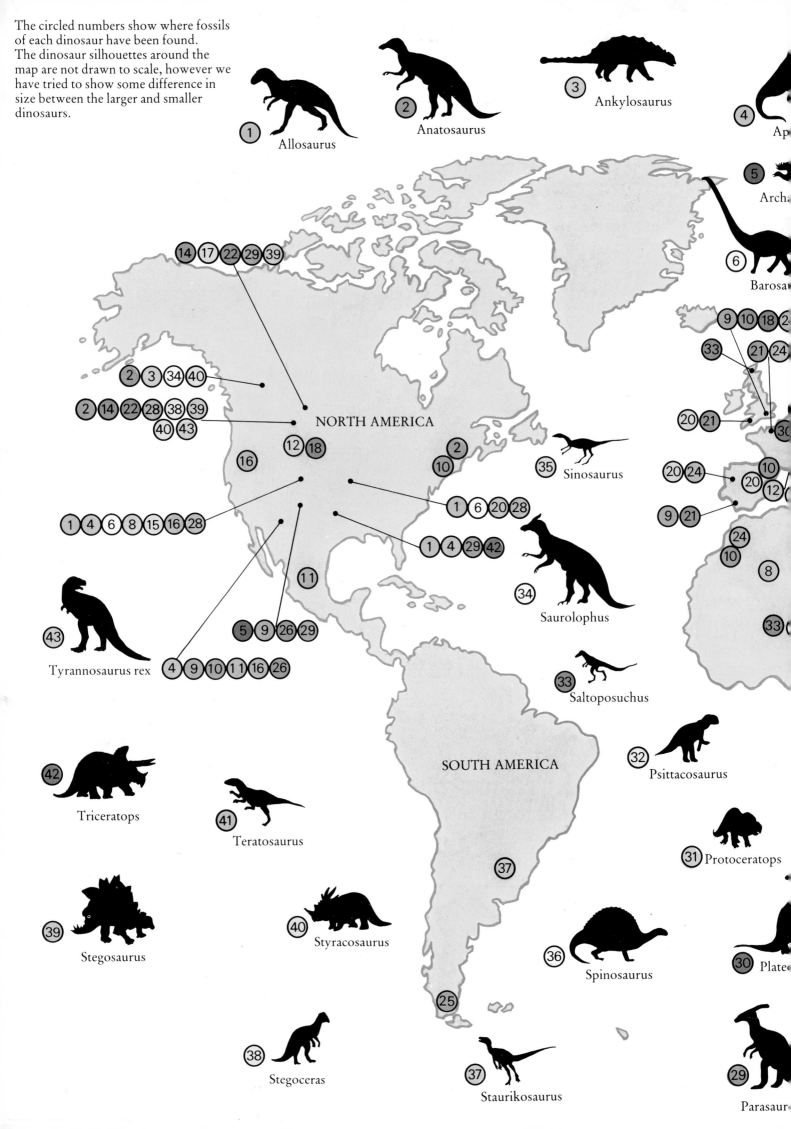

① Allosaurus

② Anatosaurus

③ Ankylosaurus

④ Ap

⑤ Archa

⑥ Barosa

NORTH AMERICA

⑭ ⑰ ㉒ ㉙ ㊴

② ③ ㉞ ㊵

② ⑭ ㉒ ㉘ ㊳ ㊴ ㊵ ㊸

⑯

⑫ ⑱

① ④ ⑥ ⑧ ⑮ ⑯ ㉘

② ⑩

① ⑥ ⑳ ㉘

① ④ ㉙ ㊷

⑪

⑤ ⑨ ㉖ ㉙

④ ⑨ ⑩ ⑪ ⑯ ㉖

⑨ ⑩ ⑱ ㉔

㉝ ㉑ ㉔

⑳ ㉑

⑳ ㉔ ⑳ ⑩ ⑫

⑨ ㉑

㉔ ⑩

⑧

㉝

㉟ Sinosaurus

㉞ Saurolophus

㉝ Saltoposuchus

㉜ Psittacosaurus

㊸ Tyrannosaurus rex

㊷ Triceratops

㊶ Teratosaurus

SOUTH AMERICA

㉛ Protoceratops

㊲ Staurikosaurus

㉚ Plate

㊴ Stegosaurus

㊵ Styracosaurus

㊱ Spinosaurus

㉞

㊲

㉕

㊳ Stegoceras

㉙ Parasaur